Peter and the Pelican

504

I0116422

Produced by Big Boot Books
Illustrated by Jacqueline Kulla

...to the children of the Gulf Coast

This is Peter.

Peter lives in a place way down at the bottom of the map, called Grand Isle, right on the coast of the Gulf of Mexico.

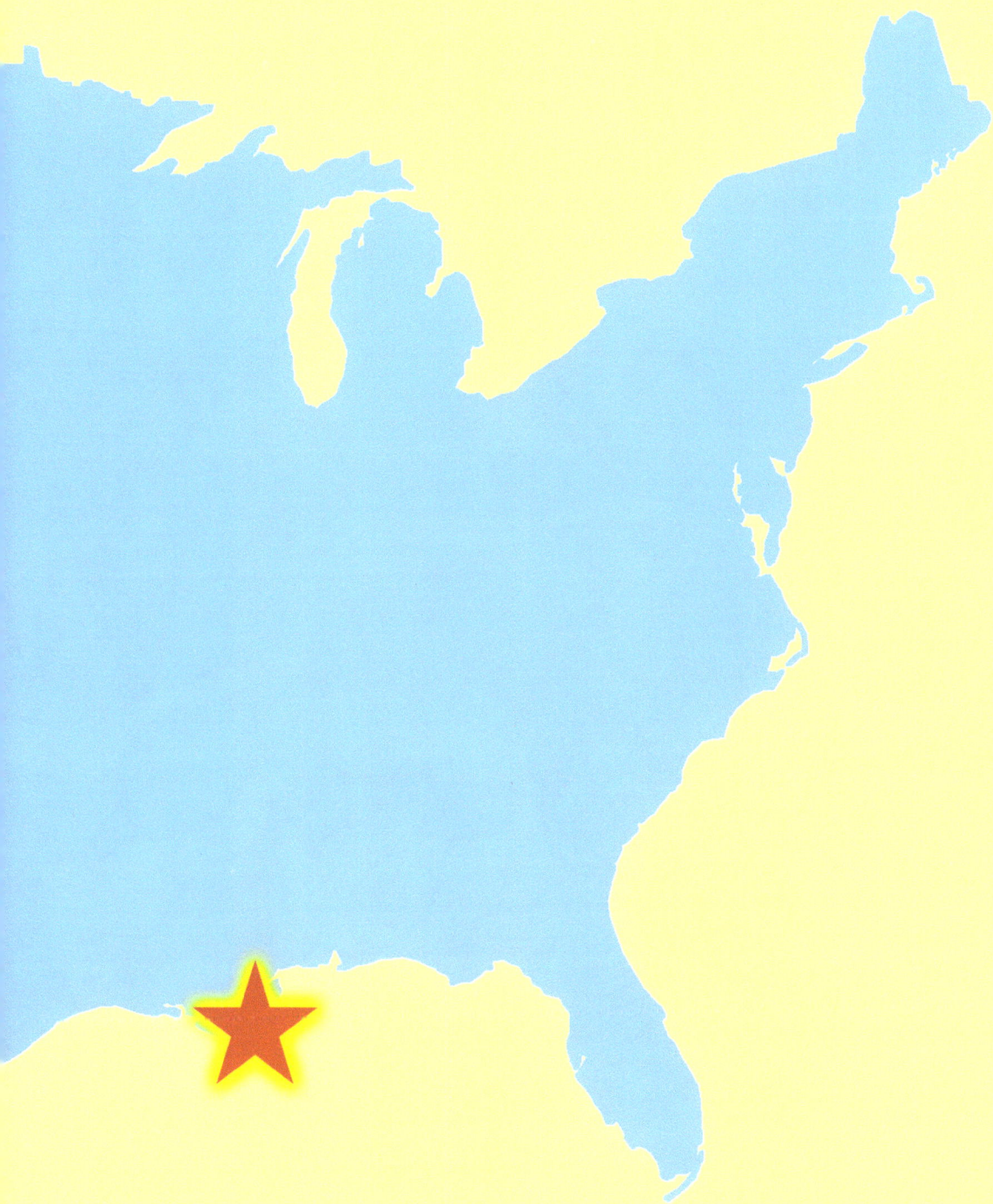

Peter's favorite thing to do was play at the park on the beach with his friends Paulina, Percy and Patricia.

They loved to feel
the cool breeze,
smell the fresh air
and hear the waves
crash along the shore
as they play.

One day, Peter got to the park and was surprised when he found a large fence surrounding the playground, with a big sign hanging from it.

PARKCLOSED
FOR DEMOLITION
DUE TO COASTAL EROSION

DONOT ENTER

A pelican was nearby and overheard the kids talking. "I know you all are upset about your park but do any of you know what coastal erosion is?" asked the pelican..

"What's coastal erosion?" asked Peter.

"Coastal erosion is when the land on the shore begins to disappear due to natural and man made actions," said the pelican.

"It's a pretty big deal and your park isn't the only thing being affected. Let's go for a ride and I'll show you more areas that are being destroyed."

"I thought you said
it was being destroyed?"
asked Patricia,
"Everything looks beautiful from
up here and all the animals look happy!"

"That's because you have to look closer,"
said the Pelican." If we lose the coast
then the pelicans and turtles won't
have anywhere to lay their eggs, the
alligators will lose their homes and
lots of trees and plants will be gone
forever! If we don't do anything,
all of this and more will be thrown
out of balance."

After their ride, the kids got together and decided that they had to do something. They wanted to help save the animals and their homes.

"Meet me here tomorrow morning," said Peter, "I have a plan!"

The next day, Peter brought a notebook filled with ideas and the kids got to work! First, they hired a local truck company to deliver sand near the park to nourish the beach.

Then, the kids built windbreaks along the shore to slow down the wind before hitting the coast.

Next, they planted seaweed below the surface to slow down water carrying sand away from the coast.

Finally, they placed breakers along the beach to stop waves from crashing onto the shore.

After all of their hard work, Peter, Patricia, Paulina and Percy, were honored by the Mayor at a ceremony in front of the entire city. All of the kids felt really good and were happy they decided to do something to combat coastal erosion in their own community.

After the ceremony, the Mayor told the kids that she had a surprise for them and asked them to follow her to the park. "Not only did your hard work help protect our coast," said the Mayor, "but your good deeds have also saved your park! Great job kids! Now get out there and play!"

After the fence was removed, all of the kids began playing. They were happy to finally be at their favorite park again, but...

...even happier to know that the pelican and his animal friends still had a beautiful place to call home.

www.ingramcontent.com/pod-product-compliance
Lightning Source LLC
Chambersburg PA
CBHW060842270326
41933CB00002B/175